AKBAR & JEFF'S GUIDE TO LIFE

A CARTOON BOOK BY MATT GROENING

OTHER BOOKS BY THE SAME CARTOONIST

LOVE IS HELL
WORK IS HELL
SCHOOL IS HELL
CHILDHOOD IS HELL

WILL IT NEVER END?

WORKS IN PROGRESS

AKBAR & JEFF'S BIG BOOK OF FEZZES
AKBAR & JEFF'S LITTLE BOOK OF FEZZES
AKBAR & JEFF'S MAKE-IT-YOURSELF FEZ BOOK
AKBAR & JEFF'S 1001 TRICKS YOU CAN DO WITH YOUR FEZ
THE SATANIC FEZZES
AKBAR & JEFF'S ENCYCLOPEDIA FEZZANNICA

FEZ! (THE NOVELIZATION)

DEDICATED TO MY SON HOMER

Copyright ©1982, 1984, 1986, 1987, 1988, 1989 by Matt Groening

All rights reserved under International and Pan-American Copyright Conventions. Published in the United States by Pantheon Books, a division of Random House, Inc., New York, and simultaneously in Canada by Random House of Canada Limited, Toronto.

I.S.B.N. 0-679-72680-2
L.C. No. 89-42647

EDITOR: WENDY WOLF
LEGAL ADVISOR: SUSAN GRODE

THANKS TO ALL AT THE LIFE IN HELL CARTOON CO./ACME FEATURES SYNDICATE: LORI ABRAMSON, DEREK BROWN, GARY BUSHERT, DIANE PIRRITINO, SANDRA ROBINSON, AND MICHELLE SHIRES

BACK COVER DESIGN: MILI SMYTHE

THE USUAL DELUXE THANKS TO THE RADIANT DEBORAH CAPLAN

IF YOU LOOK UP "FUNK QUEEN" IN THE ENCYCLOPEDIA YOU'LL SEE A PHOTO OF LYNDA BARRY IF THERE'S ANY JUSTICE IN THIS UNIVERSE. FOR INFO, WRITE TO THE LIFE IN HELL CARTOON CO., 2219 MAIN ST., SUITE E, SANTA MONICA, CA 90405, USA. PHONE: (213) 392-1619.
FAX: (213) 392-6129

Manufactured in the United States of America

First Edition

ALL-NEW
LIFE IN
HELL
MY BACK IS BETTER, THANK YOU

©1987 BY
MATT
GROENING
ON VENUS

LIFE IN HELL

LIFE IN HELL

HEY YOU!!

C'MERE.

I WANT TO KNOW SOMETHING. HOW COME YOUR PEOPLE TOOK A PERFECTLY NORMAL WORD--"GAY"-- AND RUINED IT FOR THE REST OF US?

IT'S VERY SIMPLE.

WE CALL OURSELVES GAY--

--BECAUSE WE **ARE** GAY.

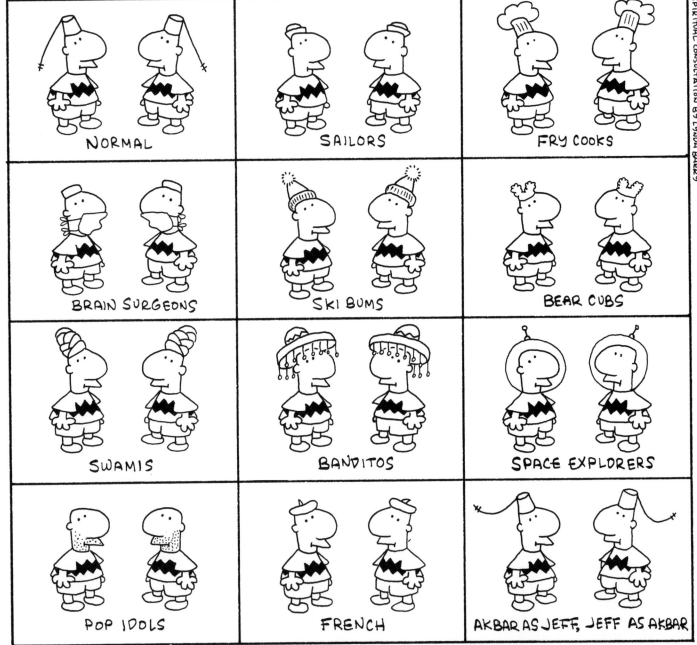

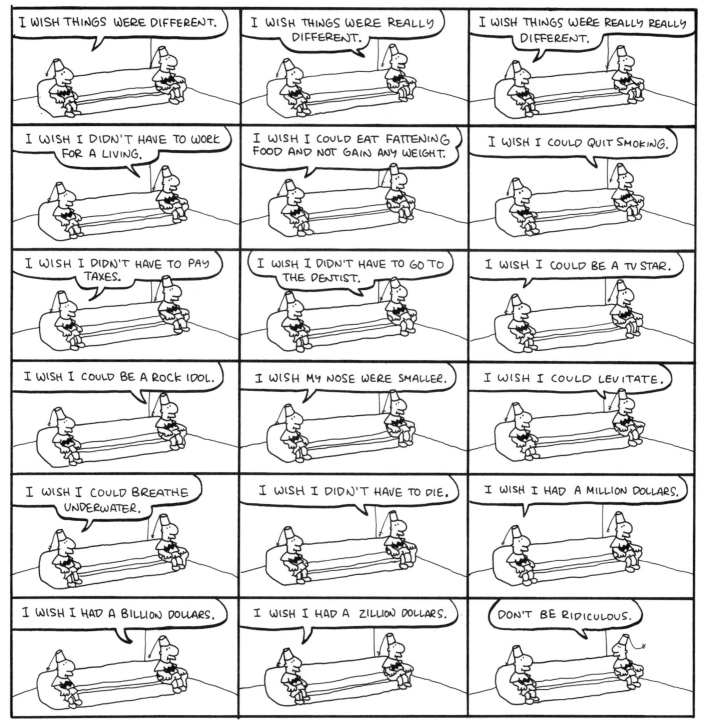

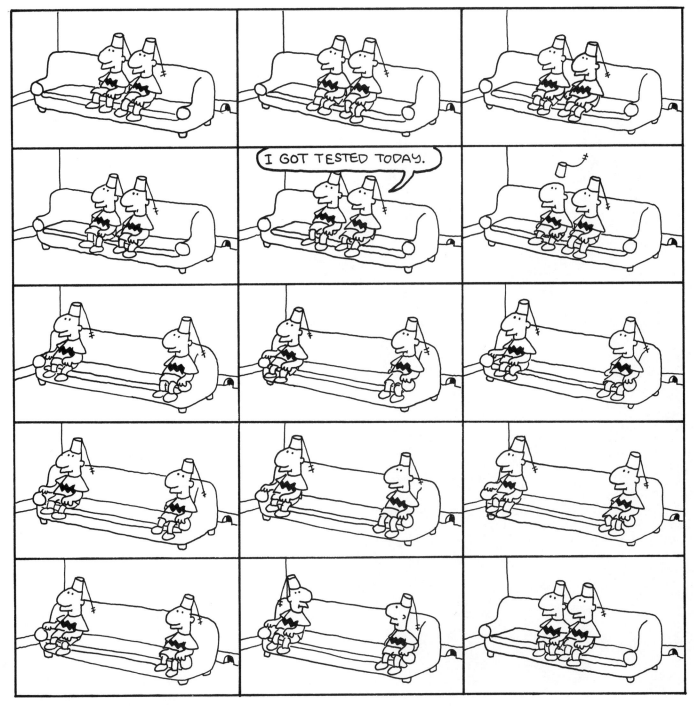

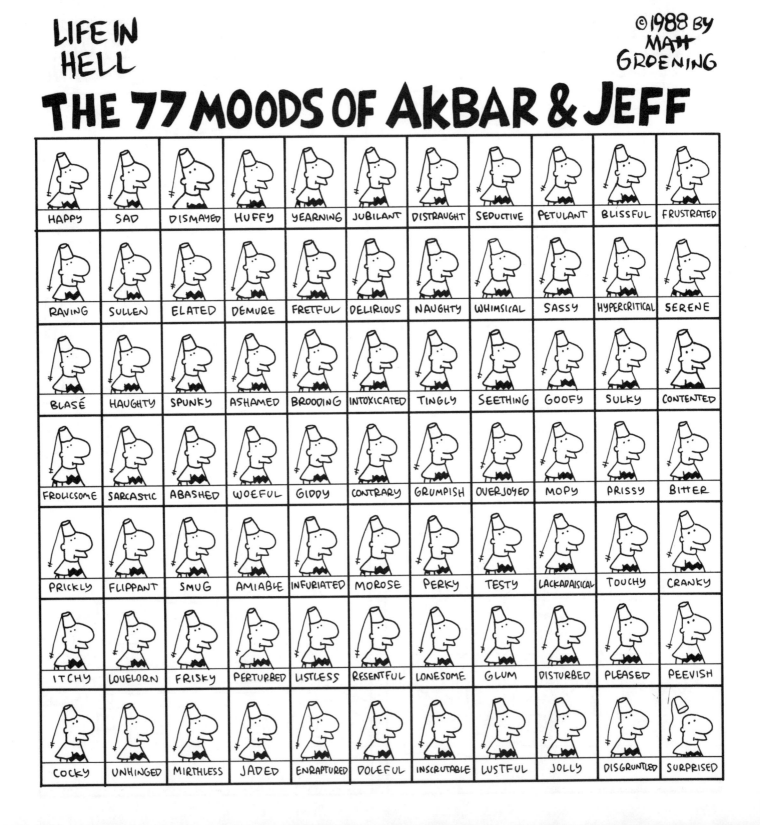

LIFE IN HELL

LIFE IN HELL

MY LIFE WITH AKBAR
BY JEFF

MY LIFE WITH AKBAR
—·—
BY JEFF

COPYRIGHT ©1989 BY JEFF. ALL RIGHTS RESERVED.

FIRST PRINTING

Dedicated to A.

TABLE OF CONTENTS

CHAPTER I
   Questions about Akbar
CHAPTER II
   Answers
CHAPTER III
   The Mystery of Akbar
CHAPTER IV
   Akbar Revealed
CHAPTER V Conclusion

CHAPTER I
Questions about Akbar

What is it about Akbar? What makes him tick? Why is he so adorable?
   These are just some of the questions I am asked every day.

CHAPTER II
Answers

If the truth be known, I never know how to answer.

CHAPTER III
The Mystery of Akbar

You see, Akbar is an enigma. He is a puzzle. You don't know what he is thinking. Maybe that is why people like him so much.

CHAPTER IV
Akbar Revealed

All I know is this: Akbar is spiritually enlightened. His fashion sense is impeccable. He is possessed of an almost canine sensuality.

He is kind, yet he is crafty. He is serene, yet he is unpredictable. He is stunningly handsome. And he is unique.

CHAPTER V
Conclusion

And that's good enough for me.

the end

IF YOU LIKED "MY LIFE WITH AKBAR," DON'T MISS

MY LIFE WITH JEFF
BY AKBAR

ON SALE EVERYWHERE

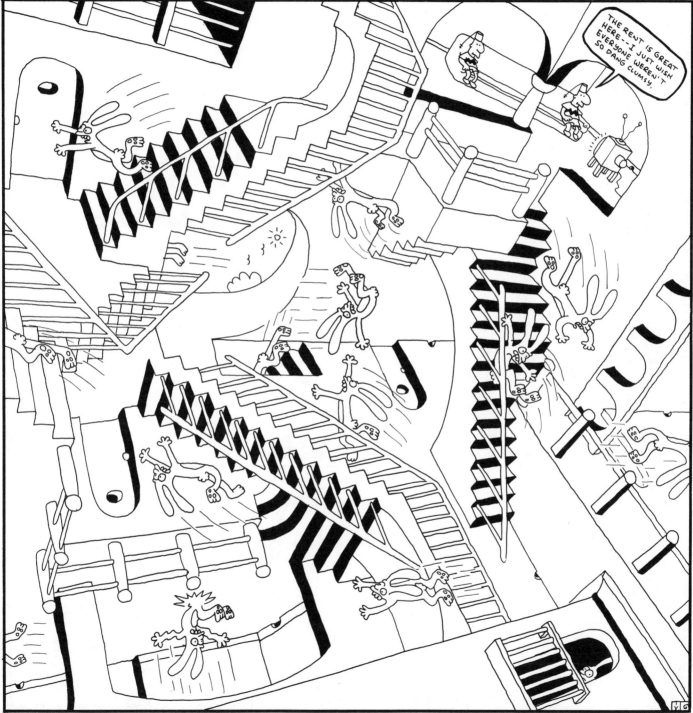

©1987 BY MATT GROENING